D0320006

The Blue Day Book

D0320006

The Blue Day Book

The Blue Day Book

A Lesson in Cheering Yourself Up

Bradley Trevor Greive

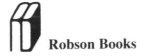

Robson Books

First published in Great Britain in 2001 by Robson Books, 10
Blenheim Court, Brewery Road, London N7 9NT

A member of the Chrysalis Group plc

Copyright © 2001 Bradley Trevor Greive
The right of Bradley Trevor Greive to be identified as author
of this work has been asserted by him in accordance with
the Copyright, Designs and Patents Act 1988

British Library Cataloguing in Publication Data
A catalogue record for this title is available from the British
Library

ISBN 1 86105 395 9

All rights reserved. No part of this publication may be
reproduced, stored in a retrieval system, or transmitted in
any form or by any means, electronic, mechanical, photo-
copying, recording or otherwise, without the prior permission in writing of the publishers.

Printed in Spain by Book Print, S.L.

To my wonderful parents, Fay and Trevor Greive,
who never stopped taking me out to see the world
even after I was bitten by penguins, twice.

Bradley Trevor Greive was born in Australia's island state of Tasmania. He has been gainfully employed as an artist, cartoonist, furniture and toy designer, animation director, screenwriter, and paratroop platoon commander. He currently lives in Sydney, and divides much of his time between Los Angeles and New York.

Acknowledgments

There are so many incredible photographs in *The Blue Day Book* that it's not possible to credit every single photographer in the space we have. But I would like to say that the magic in every image speaks of a talent and purpose that my clumsy prose could only diminish. What wonderful breed of artist could squeeze so much into a fraction of a fraction of a moment? Thank you.

A tiny book like this appears deceptively simple. It is not. I owe great thanks to the many people who encouraged me to pursue the project, particularly after the first five rejections. My adorable sisters, Linley and Vanessa, led the charge along with my dear friends Basquali Skamaachi, Siimon Reynolds, Imogen Banks, and Jane Malone. Special awards are due to Sue Greaves, Emma McClure, and Norma Scott, who let me invade their photo archives without flinching, and of course to my editor, Christine Schillig, and her team at Andrews McMeel, who turned a scribbly submission into this beautiful little book.

I am particularly grateful to Al Zuckerman, my agent at Writers House in New York, and his faithful and witty assistant, Fay Greenfield, for setting me loose in America. I also want to say a special thank-you to marketing superstar Leslie Ferraro, who personally made up about one million photocopied submissions late one San Francisco summer night so that an impoverished Australian artist could have a shot at the big league. With friends like these I cannot fail.

The Blue Day Book

Everybody has blue days.

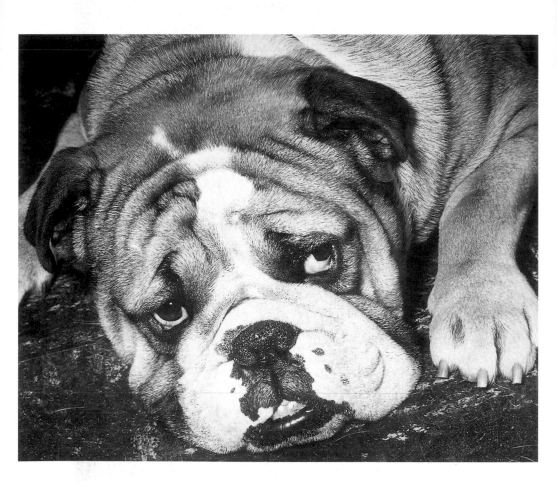

These are miserable days when you feel lousy,

grumpy,

lonely,

and utterly exhausted.

Days when you feel small and insignificant,

when everything seems just out of reach.

You can't rise to the occasion.

Just getting started seems impossible.

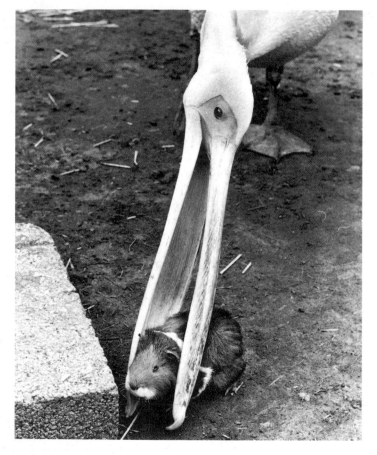

On blue days you can become paranoid
that everyone is out to get you.
(This is not always such a bad thing.)

You feel frustrated and anxious,

which can induce a nail-biting frenzy

that can escalate into a triple-chocolate-mud-cake-
eating frenzy in a blink of an eye!

On blue days you feel like you're floating
in an ocean of sadness.

You're about to burst into tears at any moment
and you don't even know why.

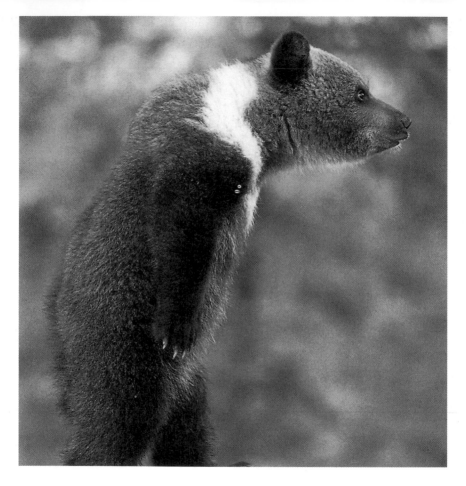

Ultimately, you feel like you're wandering
through life without purpose.

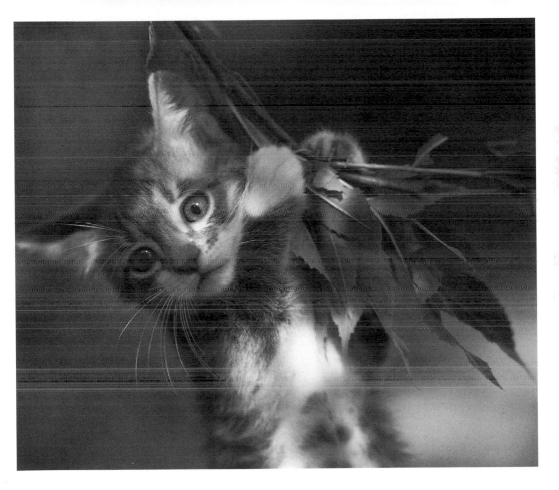

You're not sure how much longer
you can hang on,

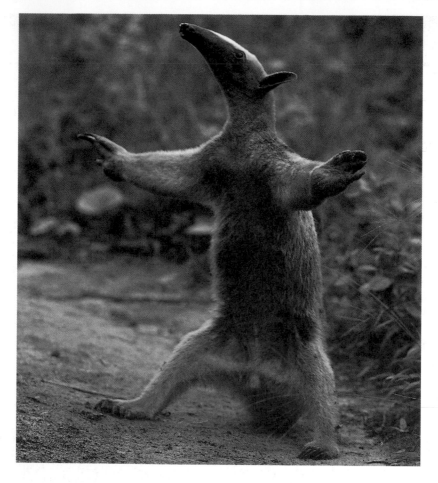

and you feel like shouting,
"Will someone please shoot me!"

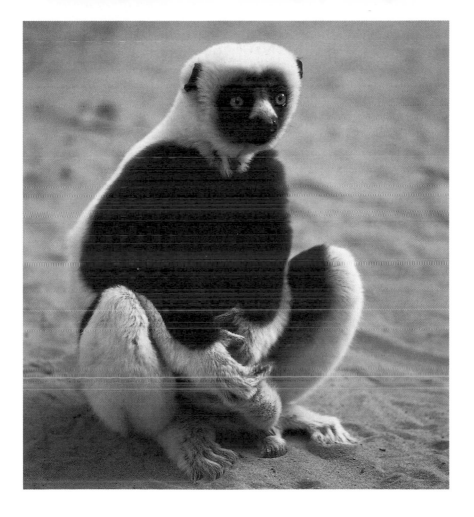

It doesn't take much to bring on a blue day.

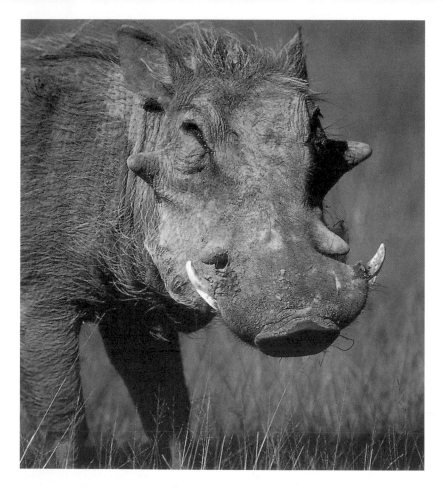

You might just wake up
not feeling or looking your best,

find some new wrinkles,

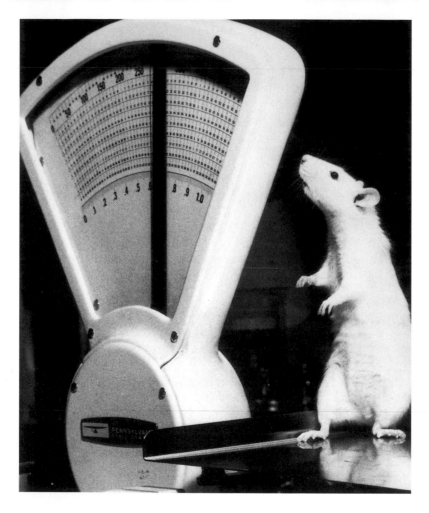

put on a little weight,

or get a huge pimple on your nose.

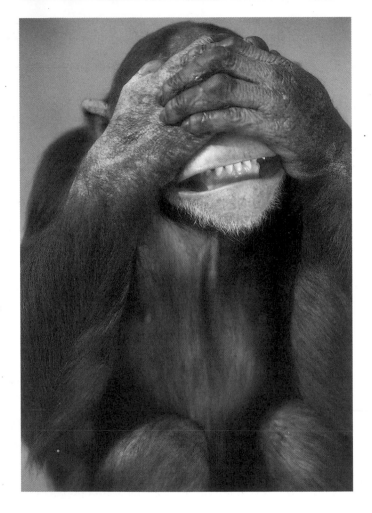

You could forget your date's name

or have an embarrassing photograph published. 25

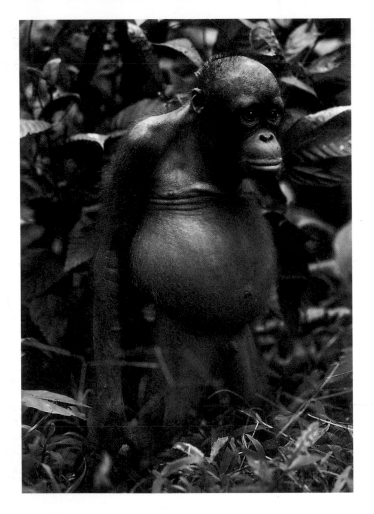

You might get dumped, divorced, or fired,

make a fool of yourself in public,

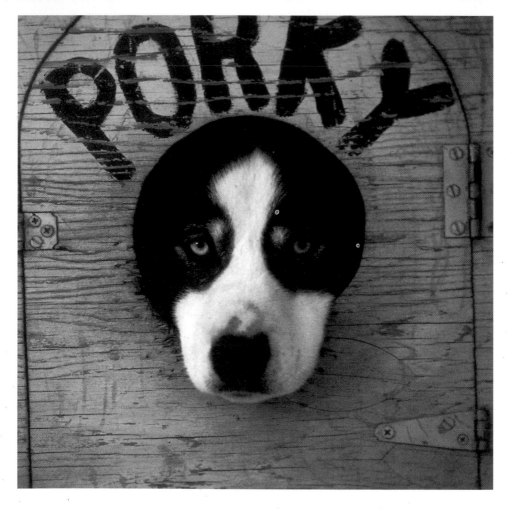

be afflicted with a demeaning nickname,

or just have a plain old bad-hair day.

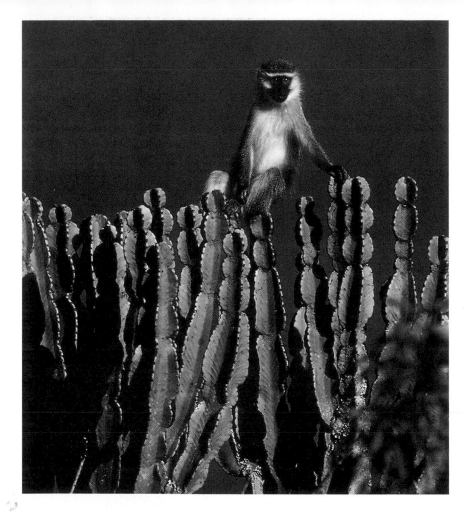

Maybe work is a pain in the butt.

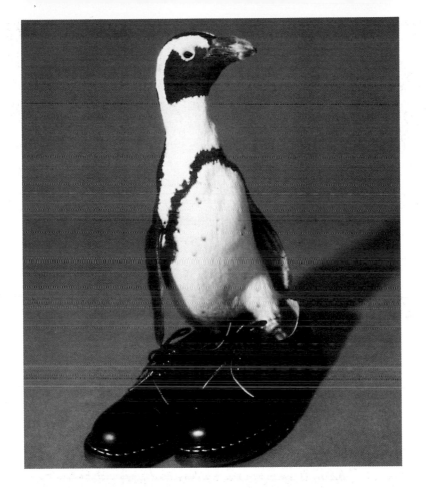

You're under major pressure
to fill someone else's shoes,

your boss is picking on you,

and everyone in the office
is driving you crazy.

33

You might have a splitting headache,

or a slipped disk,

bad breath,

a toothache,

chronic gas,

dry lips,

or a nasty ingrown toenail.

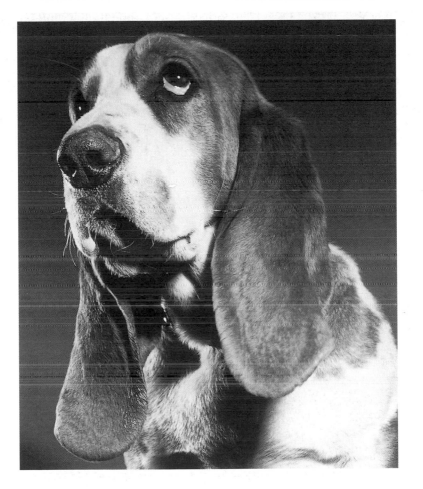

Whatever the reason, you're convinced
that someone up there doesn't like you.

Oh what to do, what to dooo?

Well, if you're like most people, you'll hide behind a
flimsy belief that everything will sort itself out.

Then you'll spend the rest of your life
looking over your shoulder, waiting for everything
to go wrong all over again.

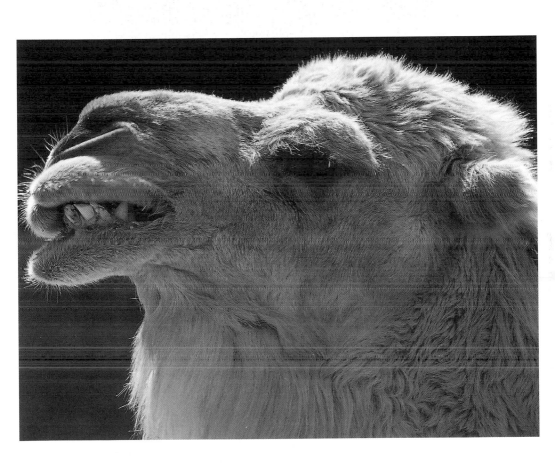

All the while becoming crusty and cynical

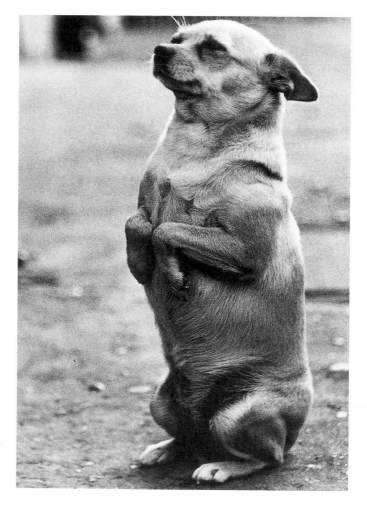

or a pathetic, sniveling victim.

Until you get so depressed that you lie down
and beg the earth to swallow you up

or, even worse, become addicted
to Billy Joel songs.

This is crazy, because you're only young once 49

and you're never old twice.

Who knows what fantastic things are in store just around the corner?

After all, the world is full
of amazing discoveries,

things you can't even imagine now.

There are delicious, happy sniffs

and scrumptious snacks to share.

Hey, you might end up fabulously rich

or even become a huge superstar (one day).

Sounds good, doesn't it?

But wait, there's more!

There are handstands

and games to play

and yoga

and karaoke

and wild, crazy, bohemian dancing.

But best of all, there's romance.

Which means long dreamy stares,

whispering sweet nothings,

cuddles,

smooches,

a frisky love bite or two,

and then, well, anything goes.

So how can you find that blissful
"just sliding into a hot bubble bath"
kind of feeling?

It's easy.

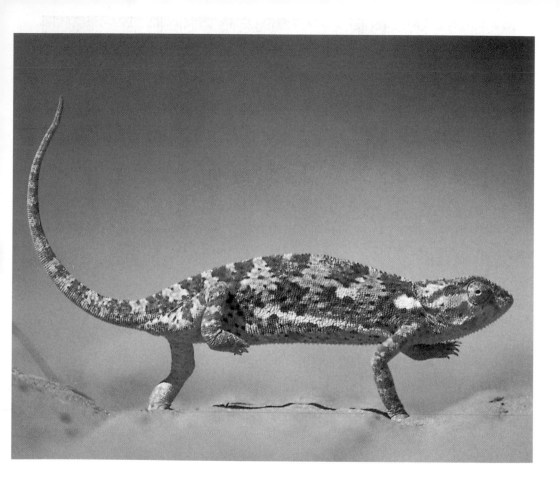

First, stop slinking away from all those nagging issues.
It's time to face the music.

Now, just relax. Take some deep breaths
(in through the nose and out through the mouth).
Try to meditate if you can.

Or go for a walk to clear your head.

Accept the fact that you'll have to let go
of some emotional baggage.

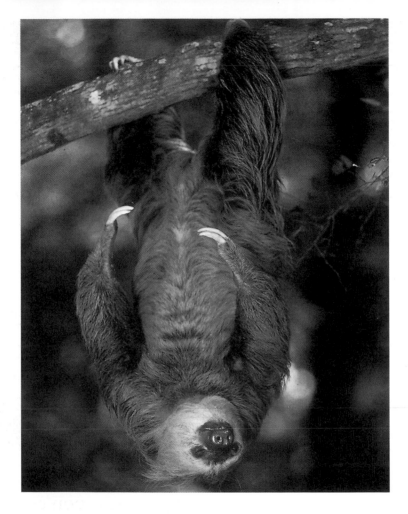

Try seeing things from a different perspective.

Maybe you're actually the one at fault.
If that's the case, be big enough to say you're sorry
(it's never too late to do this).

If someone else is doing the wrong thing,
stand up tall and say, "That's not right and I won't
stand for it!" It's okay to be forceful.

(It's rarely okay to blow raspberries.)

Be proud of who you are,

but don't lose the ability to laugh at yourself.

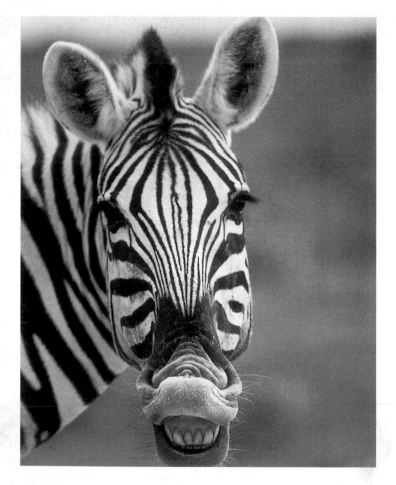

(This is a lot easier when you associate
with positive people.)

Live every day as if it were your last,
because one day it will be.

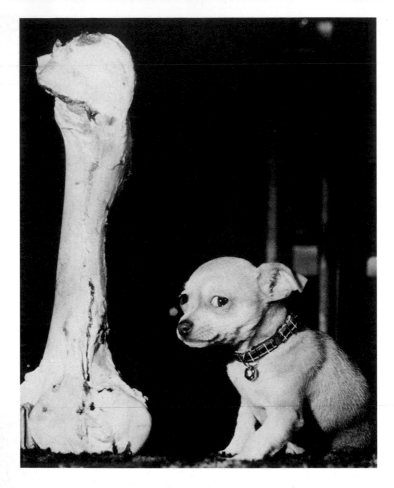

Don't be afraid to bite off
more than you can chew.

Take big risks.

Never hang back. Get out there and go for it.

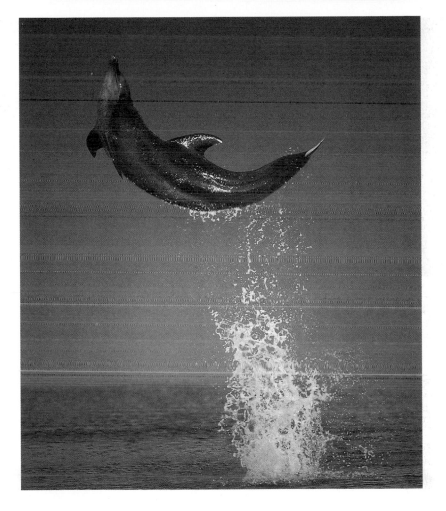

After all, isn't that what life is all about?

I think so too.

Credits:

Photographs are used with permission from the following sources:

IPL IMAGE GROUP (Sydney)
Level 2
68 Alfred Street
MILSONS POINT
NSW 2061
Australia

IPL images appear on the following pages:
Cover, 2, 3, 5, 7, 8, 10, 11, 13, 19, 21, 22, 23, 24, 25, 28, 29, 31, 32, 33, 34, 36,
37, 38, 39, 40, 41, 42, 46, 49, 50, 51, 52, 56, 57, 58, 59, 60, 61, 62, 63, 65, 68, 69,
70, 71, 75, 77, 78, 79, 81, 82, 84, 87, 88, 91, 92.

AUSTRAL INTERNATIONAL (Sydney)
Level 5
1 Chandos Street
ST LEONARDS
NSW 2065
Australia

Austral images appear on the following pages:
6, 12, 15, 17, 35, 47, 48, 89.

AUSTRALIAN PICTURE LIBRARY (Sydney)
Suite 1
2 Northcote Street
ST LEONARDS
NSW 2065
Australia

APL images appear on the following pages:
1, 4, 9, 14, 16, 18, 20, 26, 27, 30, 43, 44, 45, 53, 54, 55, 64, 66, 67, 72, 73, 74, 76,
80, 83, 85, 86, 90.